How I Learned Geography

Uri Shulevitz

FARRAR STRAUS GIROUX

NEW YORK

www.fsgkidsbooks.com

Library of Congress Cataloging-in-Publication Data
Shulevitz, Uri, date.
    How I learned geography / Uri Shulevitz.— 1st ed.
      p. cm.
    Summary: As he spends hours studying his father's world map, a young boy escapes the hunger and misery of refugee life. Based on the author's childhood in Kazakhstan, where he lived as a Polish refugee during World War II.
    ISBN-13: 978-0-374-33499-4
    ISBN-10: 0-374-33499-4
    [1. Refugees—Fiction.   2. Maps—Fiction.   3. Geography—Fiction.   4. Shulevitz, Uri, 1935– —Childhood and youth—Fiction.]   I. Title.

PZ7.S5594 Ho 2008
[E]—dc22
                                                 2007011889

In memory of my father

When war devastated the land, buildings crumbled to dust.

Everything we had was lost,
and we fled empty-handed.

We traveled far, far east
to another country,
where summers were hot
and winters were cold,

to a city of houses made of
clay, straw, and camel dung,
surrounded by dusty steppes,
burned by the sun.

We lived in a small room
with a couple we did not know.
We slept on a dirt floor.
I had no toys and no books.
Worst of all: food was scarce.

One day,

Father went to the bazaar to buy bread.

As evening approached, he hadn't returned.
Mother and I were worried and hungry.
It was nearly dark when he came home.
He carried a long roll of paper under his arm.
"I bought a map," he announced triumphantly.

"Where is the bread?" Mother asked.

"I bought a map," he said again.

  Mother and I said nothing.

"I had enough money to buy only a tiny piece of bread,
  and we would still be hungry," he explained apologetically.

"No supper tonight," Mother said bitterly. "We'll have the map instead."

I was furious.
I didn't think I would ever forgive him,
and I went to bed hungry,
while the couple we lived with
ate their meager supper.

The husband was a writer.
He wrote in silence, but, oh! how loudly he chewed.
He chewed a small crust of bread with such enthusiasm,
as if it were the most delicious morsel in the world.
I envied him his bread and wished I were the one chewing it.
I covered my head with my blanket so I would not hear him
smacking his lips with such noisy delight.

The next day, Father hung the map.
It took up an entire wall.
Our cheerless room was flooded with color.

I became fascinated by the map
and spent long hours looking at it,
studying its every detail,
and many days drawing it
on any scrap of paper that chanced my way.

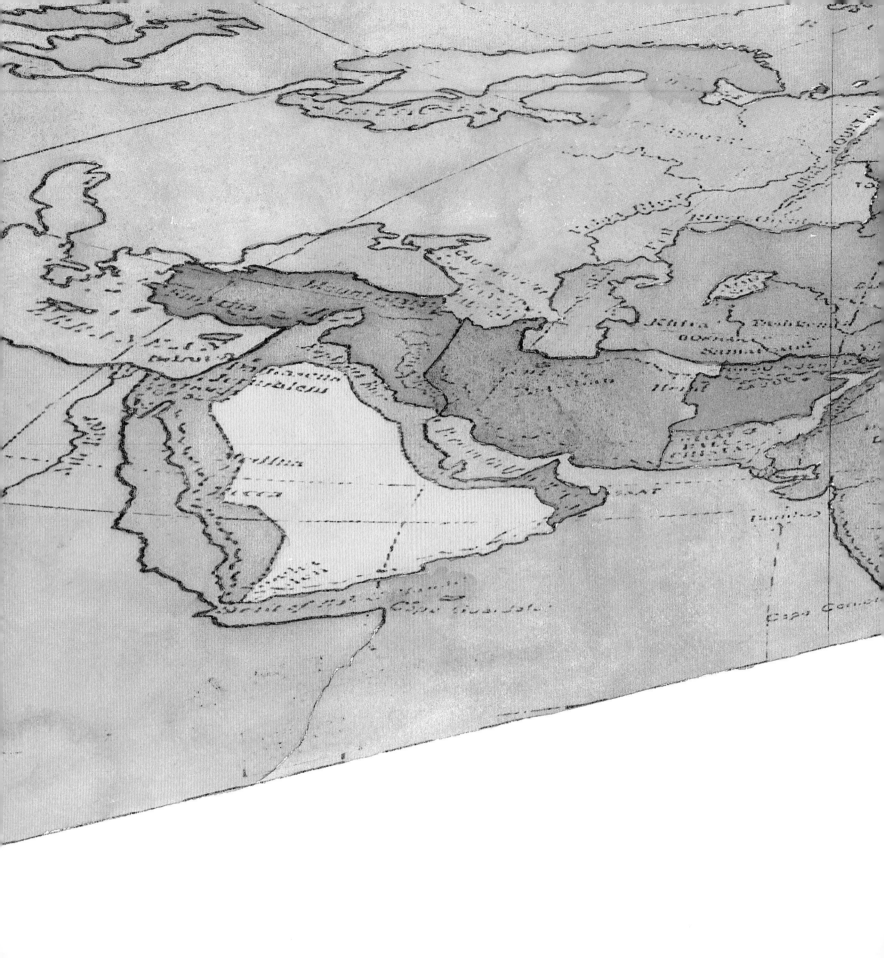

I found strange-sounding names on the map
and savored their exotic sounds,
making a little rhyme out of them:
    Fukuoka Takaoka Omsk,
    Fukuyama Nagayama Tomsk,
    Okazaki Miyazaki Pinsk,
    Pennsylvania Transylvania Minsk!
I repeated this rhyme like a magic incantation
and was transported far away without ever leaving our room.

I landed in burning deserts.

I ran on beaches and felt their sand between my toes.

I climbed snowy mountains

where icy winds licked my face.

I saw wondrous temples
where stone carvings danced on the walls,
and birds of all colors
sang on the rooftops.

I passed through fruit groves,
eating as many papayas and mangos as I pleased.

I drank fresh water
and rested in the shade of palm trees.

I came to a city of tall buildings
and counted zillions of windows,
falling asleep before I could finish.

And so I spent enchanted hours far,
far from our hunger and misery.

I forgave my father.
He was right, after all.

AUTHOR'S NOTE

Iwas born in Warsaw, Poland, in 1935. The Warsaw blitz occurred in 1939, when I was four years old. I remember streets caving in, buildings burning or crumbling to dust, and a bomb falling into the stairwell of our apartment building. Shortly thereafter, I fled Poland with my family, and for six years we lived in the Soviet Union, most of the time in Central Asia, in the city of Turkestan in what is now Kazakhstan. We eventually arrived in Paris, France, in 1947 and then moved to Israel in 1949. I came to the United States in 1959. The story in this book takes place when I was four or five years old, in the early years of our stay in Turkestan. The original map was lost long ago, so I created the maps here based on my memory of that first one, using collage, pen and ink, and watercolor.

This is me in Turkestan at age seven or eight. It is my only surviving photo at that age. I know it was taken in the winter because I'm wearing a quilted cotton jacket, which almost everyone wore during the cold months.

I drew this map of Africa at age ten on the back of a letter. I was lucky that the letter was written on one side only, because paper was a luxury and most letters were covered with writing on both sides. The map is in Russian, which I used to speak fluently, but now I can only remember a few words.

When I was thirteen, we were living in Paris, and I drew this picture of the central marketplace in Turkestan from memory. In Paris I became an avid reader of comic books, hence the cartoony style of this picture. The signs on the buildings are in Russian and mean "Barber" and "Teahouse," respectively. In those days I was a student in a French elementary school, and the lucky winner of a drawing competition held among all the elementary schools in our district. It was my first artistic success.